# Scary Creatures
# of the DEEP

D1544613

Written by
Jim Pipe

Franklin Watts®
An Imprint of Scholastic Inc.
NEW YORK • TORONTO • LONDON • AUCKLAND • SYDNEY
MEXICO CITY • NEW DELHI • HONG KONG
DANBURY, CONNECTICUT

Created and designed
by David Salariya

Author:

**Jim Pipe** studied ancient and modern history at Oxford University, and then spent ten years in publishing before becoming a full-time writer. He has written numerous nonfiction books for children, many on history and natural history. He lives in Dublin, Ireland, with his lovely wife, Melissa, and his twin boys, Daniel and Ewan.

Artists:
Mark Bergin
Carolyn Scrace
John Francis
Rob Walker

Series Creator:

**David Salariya** was born in Dundee, Scotland. In 1989 he established The Salariya Book Company. He has illustrated a wide range of books and has created many new series for publishers in the UK and overseas. He lives in Brighton, England, with his wife, illustrator Shirley Willis, and their son.

Editor: Tanya Kant

Editorial Assistant:
Rob Walker

Picture Research:
Mark Bergin, Carolyn Franklin

Photo Credits:
Deep Sea Photography

PAPER FROM
SUSTAINABLE
FORESTS

Gulper eel

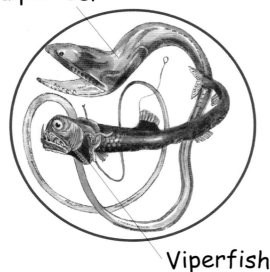

Viperfish

Created, designed, and produced by
**The Salariya Book Company Ltd**
25 Marlborough Place, Brighton BN1 1UB

A CIP catalog record for this title is available from the Library of Congress.

ISBN-13: 978-0-531-21822-8 (lib. bdg.)
978-0-531-22227-0 (pbk.)
ISBN-10: 0-531-21822-8 (lib. bdg.)
0-531-22227-6 (pbk.)

Published in 2009 in the United States by Franklin Watts
An Imprint of Scholastic Inc.
557 Broadway
New York, NY 10012

Printed in China

# Contents

Deep-sea chimaera

Fishing boat

Trawl net

Giant squid

Gulper eel

Sperm whale

submarine

## Did You Know?

The ocean deep is the least-explored place on Earth. Just 5 percent of it has been well mapped. Only two **expeditions** have ever reached the deepest part of the ocean, the Mariana Trench in the Pacific Ocean.

Deep-sea eel

Anglerfish

Light from the sun cannot reach the deepest parts of the sea, so it is always cold and dark there. Without light, no plants can grow. Yet even at the greatest depths, 6.2 miles (10 km) below the surface, the sea is home to all sorts of strange and wonderful animals.

# What Is the Ocean Deep?

If the world's oceans were drained away, you would see mountain chains and deep valleys. The tops of some of these mountains peek above the surface as islands. The bottoms of the valleys are the **ocean deep**, also called the **deep sea**. This book is about some of the strange animals that live deep in the oceans. If you're brave enough, read on!

Earth's oceans cover more than two-thirds of the planet, with an average depth of almost 2.5 miles (4 km). The deep sea has been in total darkness since there were first oceans on Earth, yet it is the planet's largest **habitat**.

5

Rattail

Sea cucumber

# Why Do Creatures of the Deep Seem Scary?

In the darkness of the ocean deep, animals need to make sure that when they catch something, it doesn't get away. Many fish have mouths stuffed with razor-sharp teeth. They look terrifying, but most are just a few inches across.

Gulper eel

Anglerfish

Snailfish

Viperfish

## Did You Know?

The gulper eel has a huge mouth, a long body, and a very elastic stomach to help it swallow and store large **prey**. Gulpers can survive for weeks without eating.

Many deep-sea fish can eat animals larger than themselves. The viperfish has a hinged skull that allows it to open its jaws incredibly wide.

7

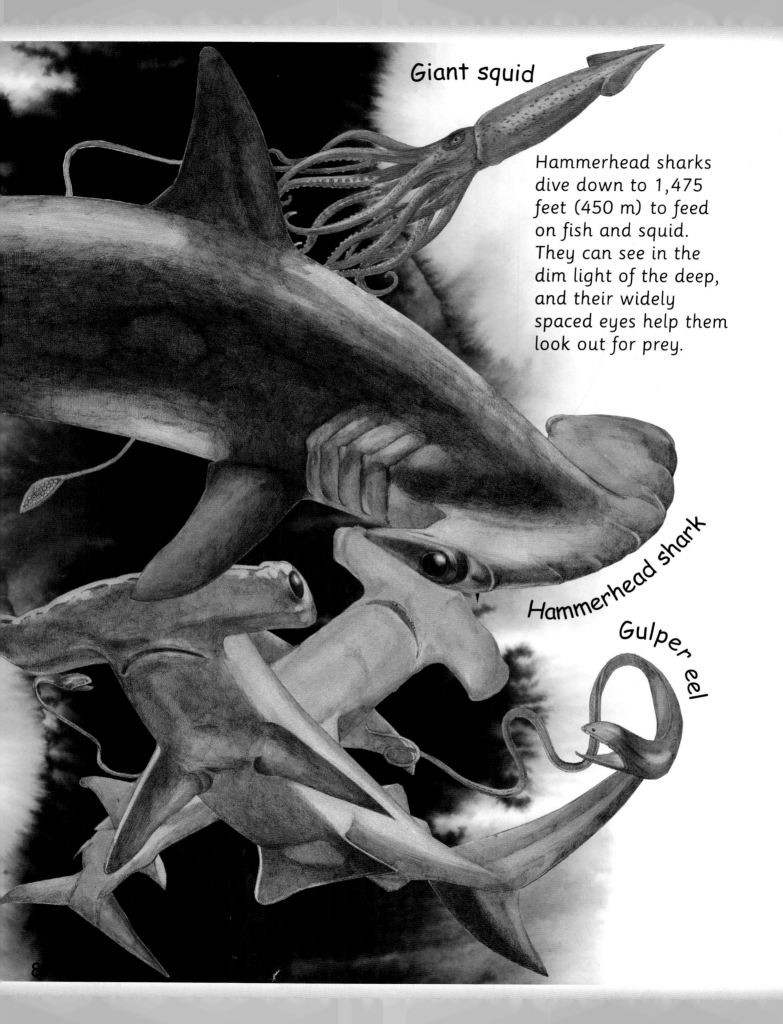

Giant squid

Hammerhead sharks dive down to 1,475 feet (450 m) to feed on fish and squid. They can see in the dim light of the deep, and their widely spaced eyes help them look out for prey.

Hammerhead shark

Gulper eel

# Why Is the Deep So Dark?

Most sea animals live near the ocean's surface, where there is plenty of sunlight. Farther down, there is still some light during the day, but the sun's rays cannot reach below about 3,300 feet (1,000 m). So the ocean deep is completely dark. It's a scary place. A **predator** can attack from above, below, or from the sides, and there's nowhere to hide!

## What is the twilight zone?

The layer of the ocean from 500 to 3,300 feet (150 to 1,000 m) below the surface is often called the **twilight zone**. Some sunlight reaches this area, but lower down the waters are dark. Many of the animals living in the twilight zone, such as luminous prawns and deep-sea shrimps, can produce their own light. This helps them blend in with the brighter waters above.

## Is the deep totally dark?

Below 3,300 feet (1,000 m), the only light in the water is the sudden flashes made by those animals that can give off light. Though they are no brighter than moonlight, these flashes seem very bright in the pitch-black ocean depths.

### Did You Know?

The barreleye fish has two big eyes that can pick up faint traces of light in the dark deep-sea waters.

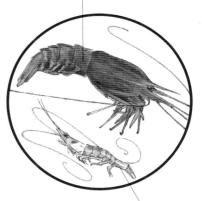
Luminous prawn

Deep-sea shrimp

Barreleye fish

# Do Deep-Sea Creatures Ever Swim to the Surface?

Some do! They swim up at night to feed at the surface, where there is plenty of food. During the day, they live in the dark depths to avoid predators that would easily catch them in the sunlit surface waters. Some shrimps travel more than 3,300 feet (1,000 m) up and down each day. They are very sensitive to light, so they stay far below the surface during the day.

**Lantern fish**

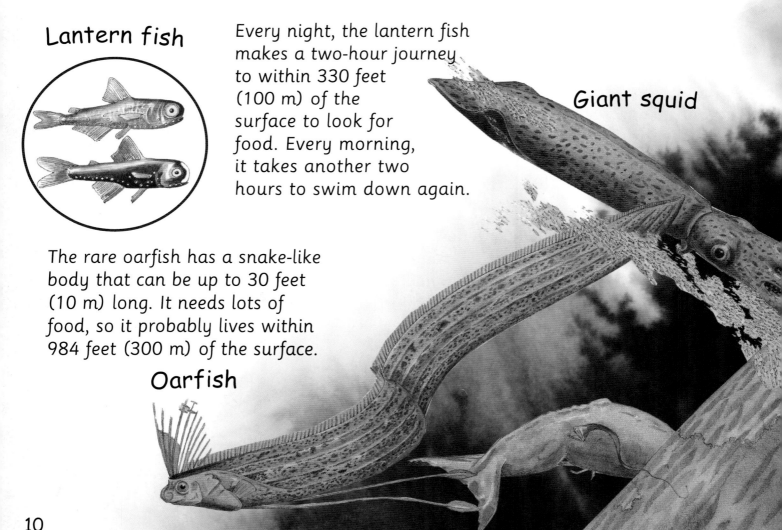

Every night, the lantern fish makes a two-hour journey to within 330 feet (100 m) of the surface to look for food. Every morning, it takes another two hours to swim down again.

**Giant squid**

The rare oarfish has a snake-like body that can be up to 30 feet (10 m) long. It needs lots of food, so it probably lives within 984 feet (300 m) of the surface.

**Oarfish**

## Did You Know?

Sperm whales can be 65 feet (20 m) long. The sperm whale takes a huge breath and then dives 1.24 miles (2 km) underwater to hunt for giant squid. These squid can be 53 feet (16 m) long, so it's a battle of the giants!

Sperm whales

# What Lives at the Bottom?

Slow-moving animals such as sea cucumbers, starfish, and sea anemones live on the ocean floor. They sit and wait for food to drop near them. Most food for deep-sea creatures comes from the surface. How does it reach the animals 6.2 miles (10 km) below? It sinks. When a whale dies, its body drops to the bottom.

Sea cucumbers live in the thick gray ooze that covers much of the ocean floor. They breathe through their bottoms and can spew out their guts to scare off predators!

## X-Ray Vision

Hold the next page up to the light and see what happens to the whale's body.

**See what's inside**

Brittle stars, worms, and limpets carpet the **seabed.**

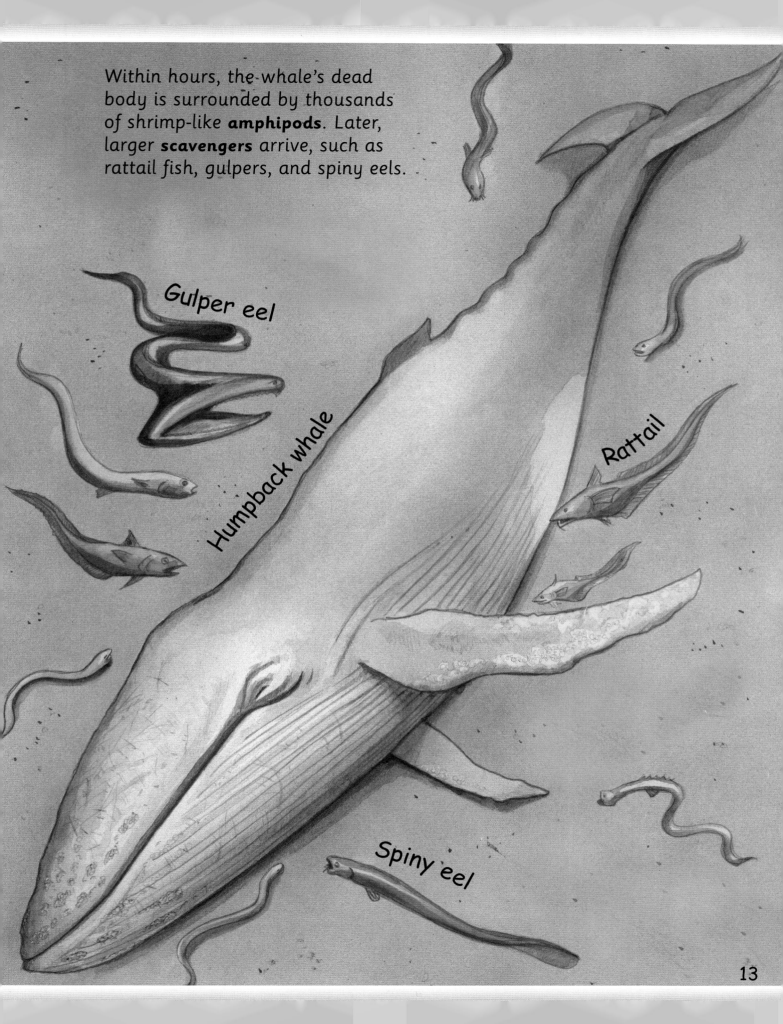

Within hours, the whale's dead body is surrounded by thousands of shrimp-like **amphipods**. Later, larger **scavengers** arrive, such as rattail fish, gulpers, and spiny eels.

Gulper eel

Humpback whale

Rattail

Spiny eel

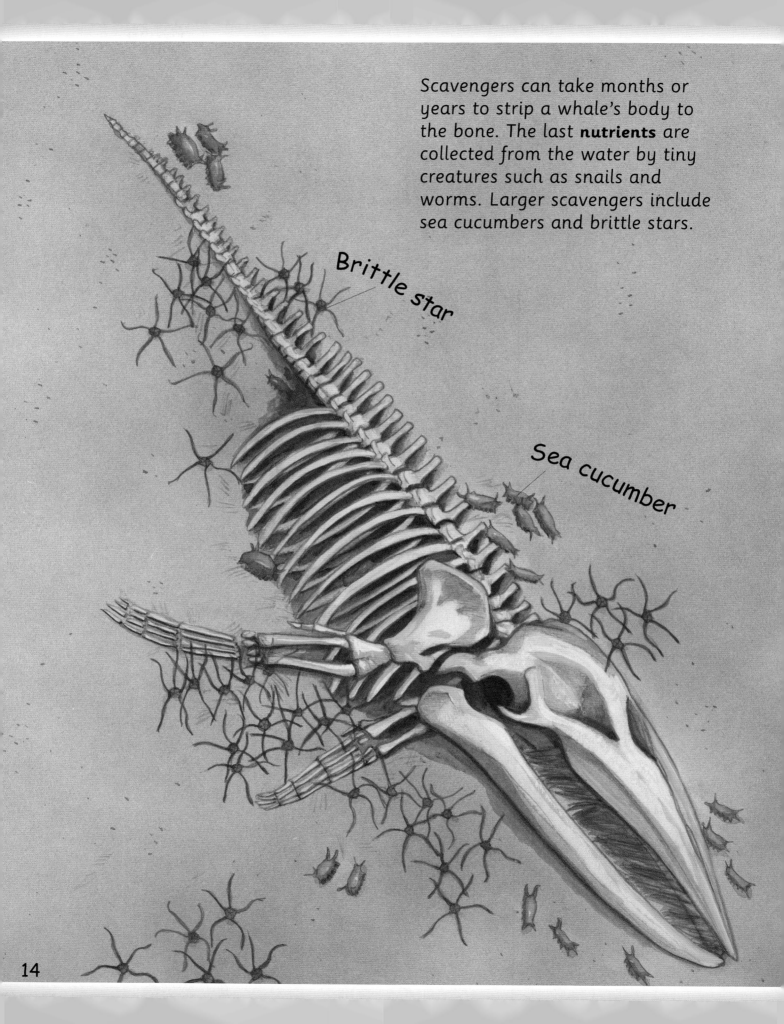

Scavengers can take months or years to strip a whale's body to the bone. The last **nutrients** are collected from the water by tiny creatures such as snails and worms. Larger scavengers include sea cucumbers and brittle stars.

Brittle star

Sea cucumber

# Why Do Some Animals Have Jelly-like Bodies?

In the deep ocean, animals are surrounded on all sides by water. Many quick-moving animals can survive without skeletons because the water supports the weight of their bodies. So jelly-bodied animals such as jellyfish and comb jellies are common.

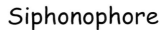

Siphonophore

When it bumps into something, the jelly-like siphonophore glows with a bright blue light. Giant siphonophores are up to 130 feet (40 m) long—that's longer than a blue whale!

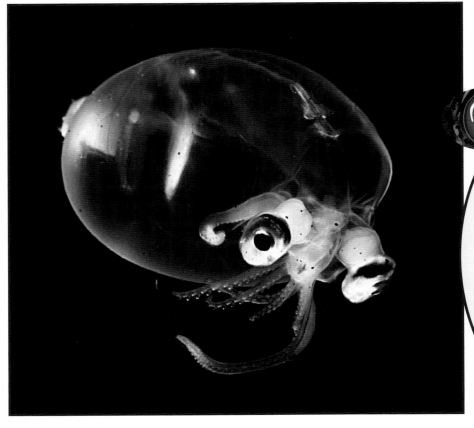

Deep-sea glass squid

## Did You Know?

Soft bodies are tempting to predators. Animals like the glass squid have almost transparent (see-through) bodies, so predators will look straight through them!

# What Sea Creatures Use Jets to Get Around?

While fish use their tails and fins to swim, squids use jet power. They suck water into their bodies, then shoot it out through a tube called a **siphon**. They can move in different directions by changing the direction of the siphon.

The sea angel hunts sea snails with a tongue studded with tiny, sharp teeth. Its mouth is at the top of its head.

Tongue

Sea angel

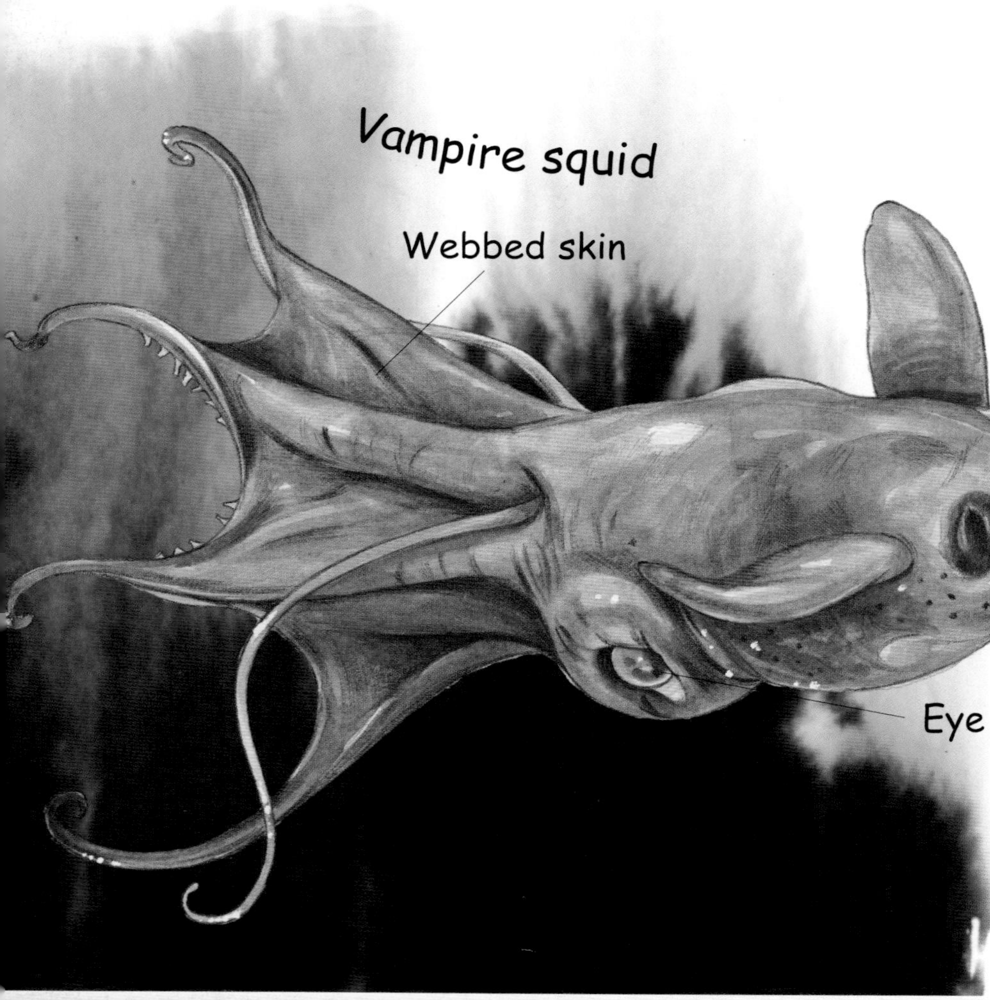

Vampire squid

Webbed skin

Eye

The vampire squid looks scary because of its big eyes and red color.
Its name comes from the webbed skin between its arms, which looks like the skin covering a bat's wing.

Many other strange-looking squids live in the deep sea. The piglet squid has a pig-like snout and holds its **tentacles** over its head. The cockatoo squid has tentacles on its head that look like a tuft of feathers.

Tentacles

Piglet squid

## Did You Know?

The vampire squid is not a true squid. It is like a squid in some ways and like an octopus in others. Like a squid, it has eight arms and two tentacles. Like an octopus, it hangs in the water by drooping its arms in an umbrella shape.

Dumbo octopus

Dumbo octopuses have two fins that look a bit like elephant ears.

# Why Do Deep-Sea Fish Look So Strange?

Deep-sea fish look strange to us because they have adapted to life in the depths. Anglerfish and fangtooths use their huge mouths to eat any prey they can find. Other deep-sea fish are long and thin so that they can cut through the water without using too much energy.

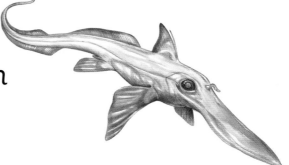

**Deep-sea chimaera**
This strange fish uses its long snout to scan the sea floor. It can sense prey buried in the mud.

Deep-sea anglerfish

**Did You Know?**

Deep-sea fish are often black, dark gray, or brown. Deep-sea fish can't attract a mate using bright colors, like the fish in a sunlit coral reef can, because there is very little light to see by.

Fangtooth or "ogrefish"

# Why Do Sea Creatures Glow?

On land, a few creatures such as fireflies and glowworms can make their own light. But in the darkness of the deep sea, 90 percent of **species**, from tiny **bacteria** to fish and squid, can make light. This is called **bioluminescence**. Some fish use flashes of light to confuse predators, while others use light to attract prey or a mate.

## X-Ray Vision

Hold the next page up to the light and see what glows in the ocean deep.

See what's inside

### How do they do it?

Sea creatures create light with special chemicals in their bodies. Most produce a blue light, but some produce green or yellow light. A few even produce red light.

### What fish goes fishing?

The dragonfish has light organs along the sides of its body. It uses these organs to attract a mate and to lure fish from deep below. Like the anglerfish, it also has a light at the end of a "fishing rod," which flashes on and off to lure prey. When a fish gets close enough, the dragonfish snaps it up in its powerful jaws.

Scaly dragonfish

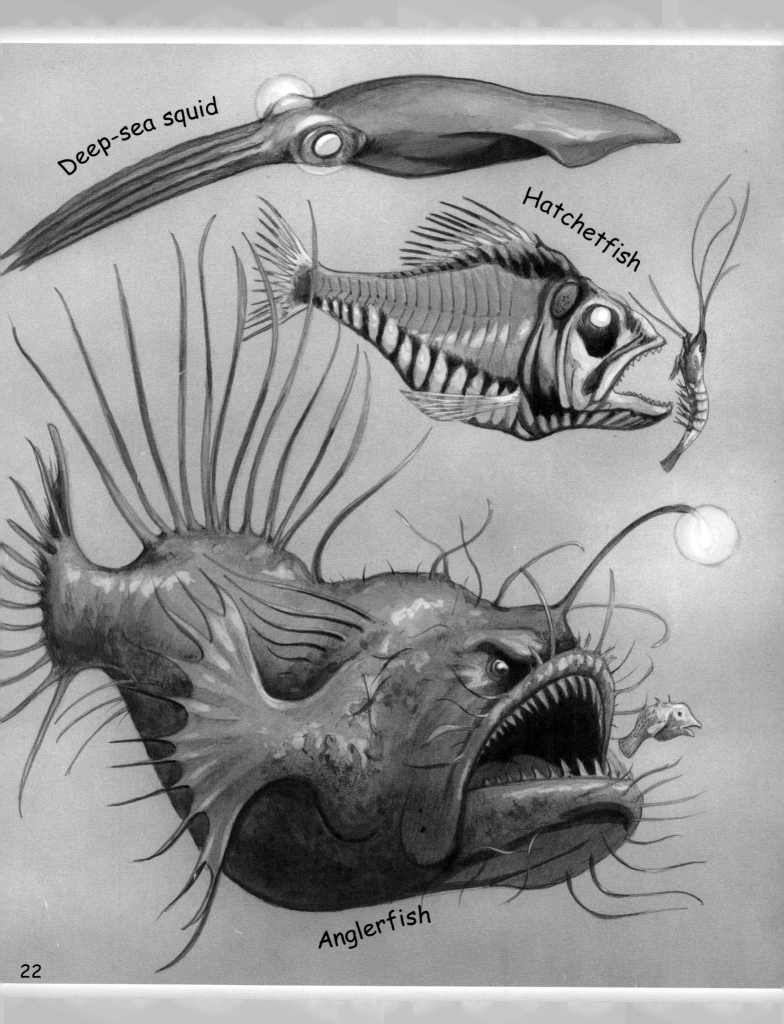

Deep-sea squid

Hatchetfish

Anglerfish

# Are There Really Sea Monsters?

No, sea monsters don't exist, despite old sailors' tales of giant, man-eating sea creatures like the Kraken pictured below. In fact, most deep-sea animals are small. The fish that live in the greatest depths, snailfish, are rarely longer than 14 inches (35 cm).

## Did You Know?

The Greenland shark is 23 feet (7 m) long and has been seen at depths of 7,200 feet (2,200 m). It also comes to the surface to catch prey. An entire reindeer was once found in a Greenland shark's stomach!

The closest thing to a real sea monster is probably the giant squid. A giant squid couldn't sink a ship, but it's a fast swimmer that uses its long tentacles to grab onto prey. It has powerful jaws like a parrot's beak and eyes the size of dinner plates.

Mythical Kraken

Anglerfish are small but scary!

# What Is Smoking at the Bottom of the Ocean?

Most of the water at the bottom of the sea is a chilly 35.6 to 37.4°F (2 to 3°C). But in the 1970s, scientists got a shock when they discovered springs of hot water, up to 750°F (400°C), gushing from the seabed. These chimney-like **vents**, called "black smokers," are made of hardened minerals. They release murky clouds of chemicals.

Black smokers help support entire deep-sea communities. The chemicals from smokers would poison most creatures, but tiny bacteria use them to make food. Shrimp-like amphipods feed on the bacteria. Then bigger animals, such as huge clams and giant spider crabs, eat the amphipods.

Giant tube worms

## Scaleworm

Tube worms are almost 6.6 feet (2 m) long and are as thick as your wrist. They grow in clusters near the vents. They have no mouths or stomachs, but get nutrients from bacteria that live inside their bodies.

## Did You Know?

Other strange animals found near undersea vents include snipe eels and vent shrimps. Snipe eels have unusual bird-like beaks. Instead of normal eyes, vent shrimps have pairs of organs on their backs that detect heat.

Hot-water vent

Giant tube worms

Small scaleworms live among the giant tube worms near the tips of smokers.

Rattail

Snipe eel

Sea cucumbers

# How Do You Explore the Ocean Deep?

Some of the most amazing discoveries of the last 100 years have taken place in the ocean's depths. Scientists find new species by using huge nets that "fly" through the water, 3 miles (5 km) below the surface. They also lower video cameras and electronic sensors from ships to gather information. Mini-submarines and unmanned robots can carry cameras and other equipment to the sea floor.

## How deep did they go?

In 1960, Jacques Piccard and Don Walsh reached the deepest point in the ocean, the Mariana Trench. It took five hours for their **bathyscaphe**, the *Trieste*, to sink almost 7 miles (11 km). They forgot to take a camera!

Bathyscaphe

Jason Jr.

A robot **submersible** called *Jason* can dive to 21,385 feet (6,500 m) to take photographs and collect small animals from the seabed. A similar submersible, *Jason Jr.*, was used to explore the wreck of the famous ocean liner, the *Titanic*.

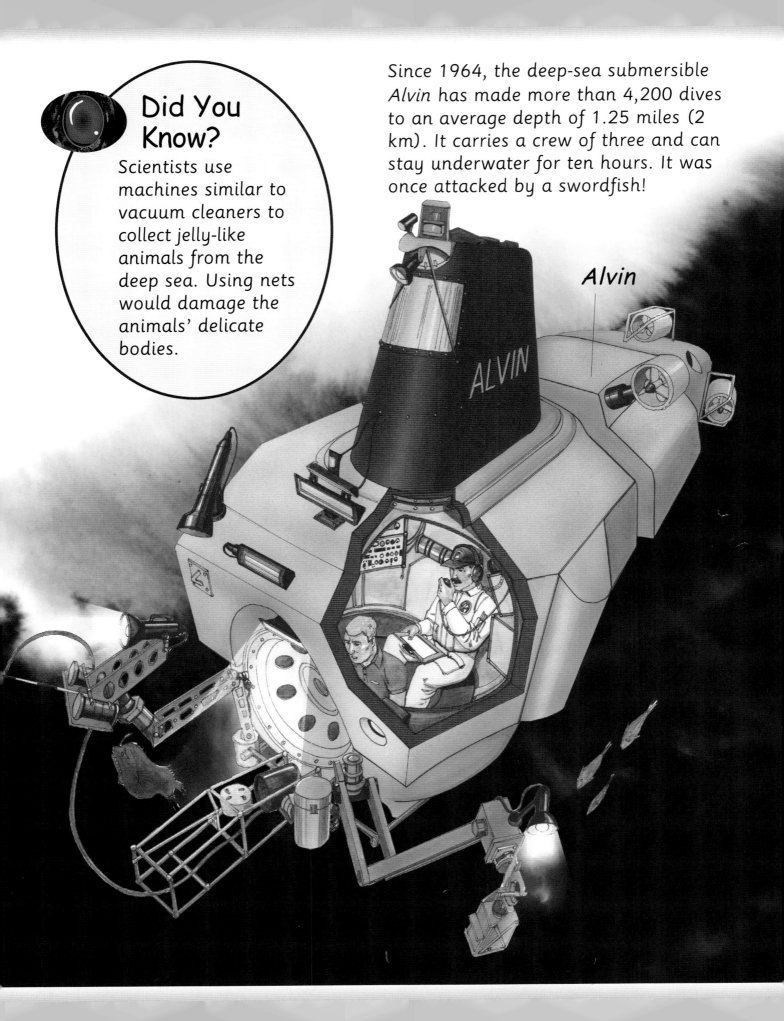

## Did You Know?

Scientists use machines similar to vacuum cleaners to collect jelly-like animals from the deep sea. Using nets would damage the animals' delicate bodies.

Since 1964, the deep-sea submersible *Alvin* has made more than 4,200 dives to an average depth of 1.25 miles (2 km). It carries a crew of three and can stay underwater for ten hours. It was once attacked by a swordfish!

*Alvin*

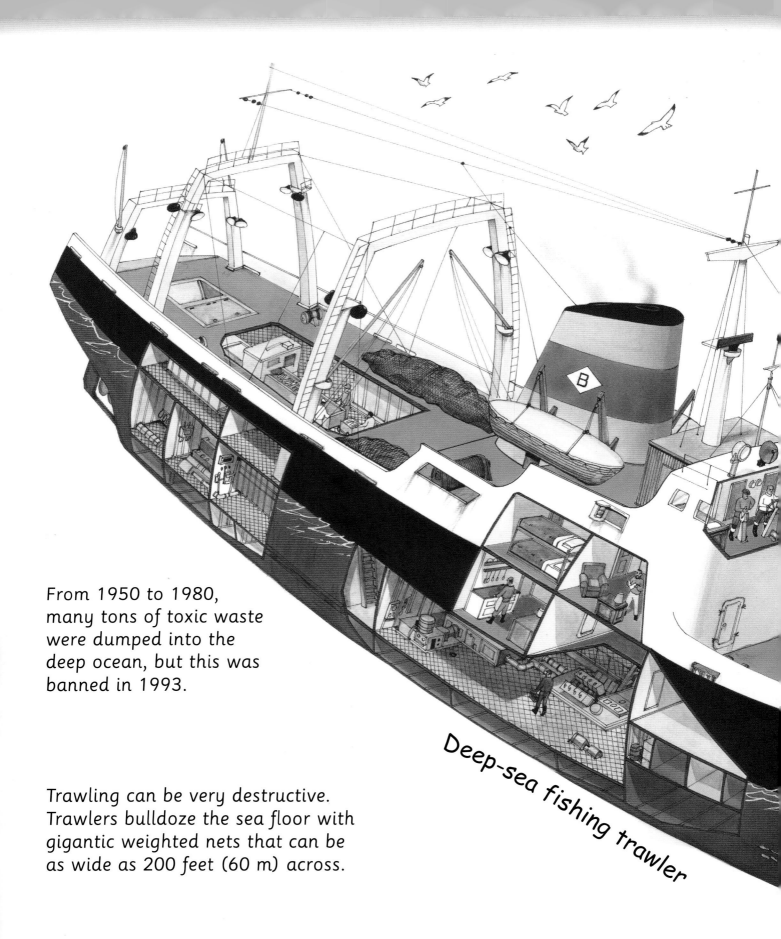

From 1950 to 1980, many tons of toxic waste were dumped into the deep ocean, but this was banned in 1993.

Trawling can be very destructive. Trawlers bulldoze the sea floor with gigantic weighted nets that can be as wide as 200 feet (60 m) across.

Deep-sea fishing trawler

# Why Should We Preserve the Deep-Sea Habitat?

We know now that the deep sea is full of life, and it's important that we protect this habitat. Nowadays, fishing fleets use huge trawl nets to catch fish at very great depths. **Trawling** has already destroyed half of the deep-water coral off Norway. The deep-sea habitat is also threatened by companies searching for valuable **ores**, minerals, and oil under the seabed.

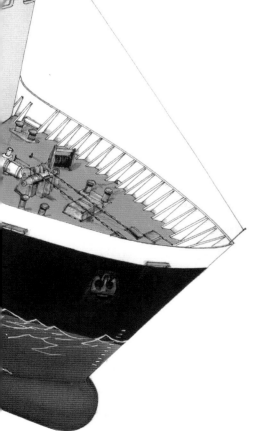

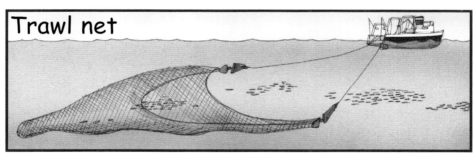

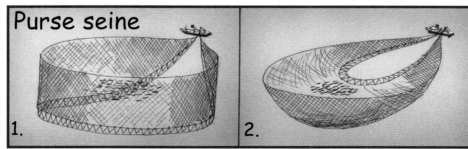

Modern fishing boats use specially shaped nets (shown above) that can catch thousands of fish at a time.

# Deep-Sea Facts

Because they are deep as well as wide, oceans make up 99 percent of the space where animals can live on Earth. 85 percent of this is the deep sea, the biggest habitat on our planet.

On average, a new deep-sea species is found every two weeks. Scientists believe there may be millions more waiting to be discovered.

The temperature at the bottom of the ocean is a brain-numbing 35–37°F (2–3°C). The water from deep sea vents is a roasting 750°F (400°C)! However, just one meter away from the vent opening, the temperature drops to 40°F (5°C).

The Japanese robot submersible *Kaiko* could dive more than 32,800 feet (10,000 m) deep, but it was lost at sea in 2003. The manned French submersible *Nautile* can reach depths of 19,700 feet (6,000 m).

At 492 feet (150 m) below the surface, 99 percent of the light from the sun is blocked by the water above. Below 3,300 feet (1,000 m), it is pitch-black.

The gigantic chimneys of black smokers can grow up to 130 feet (40 m) tall. They are formed from dissolved minerals in the hot water that harden when the hot water hits the cold seawater. One 130-foot (40-m) chimney in the Pacific Ocean was known as Godzilla before it toppled over.

The deeper you go in the sea, the more pressure, or squeezing force, there is. Around 32,800 feet (10,000 m) below the surface, the pressure is a thousand times what it is at the surface. But because the bodies of most sea creatures at that depth are made up mostly of water, they do not feel this pressure.

The deepest-living fish is a type of snailfish. One was caught at a depth of 23,720 feet (7,230 m) in the Pacific.

The heaviest creature in the deep is the sperm whale, which weighs 15.4 tons (14 metric tons). The longest is the giant siphonophore. It can grow up to 130 feet (40 m) long. Though it looks like one animal, the giant siphonophore is actually a colony of many animals, all working together.

Perhaps the strangest deep-sea creature is the jewel squid. Its body looks like a giant strawberry. It has one big eye that looks upward at sunlit areas, while a smaller eye looks down into the inky darkness below.

In 2005, a crab with hairy legs, nicknamed the "Yeti Crab," was found by *Alvin* near deep-sea vents in the Pacific Ocean off Easter Island.

# Glossary

**amphipod**  A member of a group of **crustaceans** that includes shrimps, sea lice, and sand fleas.

**bacteria**  Tiny organisms that usually consist of a single cell.

**bathyscaphe**  A type of deep-sea submersible.

**bioluminescence**  Light produced by animals' bodies, such as the glow from a firefly or an anglerfish.

**crustacean**  An animal such as a shrimp or crab, that has a hard outer shell and jointed limbs. They usually live in water and breathe using gills.

**deep sea**  The dark, cold bottom layer of the sea, more than 3,300 feet (1,000 m) below the surface. It is also known as the abyss.

**expedition**  A journey planned especially for exploration or research.

**habitat**  The natural home of a plant or animal.

**nutrient**  A substance or chemical in food that provides energy or helps animals or plants grow.

**ocean deep**  see **deep sea**

**ore**  A type of rock from which metals can be extracted.

**predator**  An animal that hunts other animals for food.

**prey**  An animal that is hunted for food.

**scavenger**  An animal that eats the dead remains and waste of plants and other animals.

**seabed**  The bottom of the sea, also called the ocean floor.

**siphon**  The tube-like part of a squid that squirts water in order to push the squid through the sea.

**species**  A group of animals or plants that look the same, live in the same way, and produce young that do the same.

**submersible**  A small underwater vessel that is launched from a larger ship.

**tentacles**  Long, flexible, arm-like organs; they often have suckers or hooks to help capture food.

**trawling**  Catching large numbers of fish using giant nets pulled behind a fishing boat.

**twilight zone**  The middle layer of the sea, from 492 feet (150 m) below the surface down to 3,300 feet (1,000 m).

**vents**  Also known as hydrothermal (hot-water) vents or black smokers. Created by underwater volcanoes, vents spew out clouds of black smoke.

# Index

Dumbo octopus